LEE EVANS ARRANGES HOLIDAY JAZZ

ISBN 978-0-634-02016-2

HAL•LEONARD®
CORPORATION
7777 W. BLUEMOUND RD. P.O. BOX 13819 MILWAUKEE, WI 53213

Visit Hal Leonard Online at
www.halleonard.com

CONTENTS

THE CHRISTMAS SONG
(CHESTNUTS ROASTING ON AN OPEN FIRE)

Music and Lyric by MEL TORME
and ROBERT WELLS
Arranged by LEE EVANS

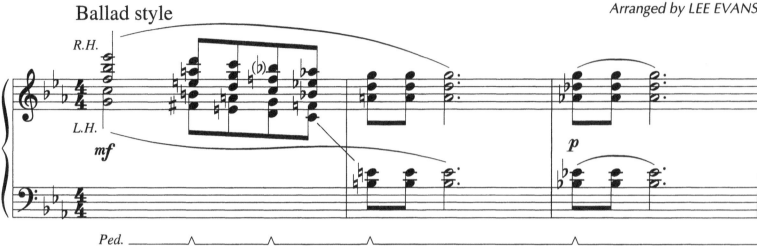

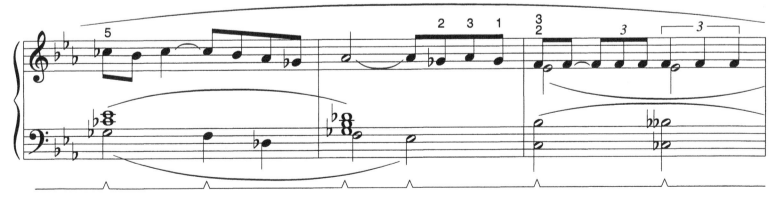

6

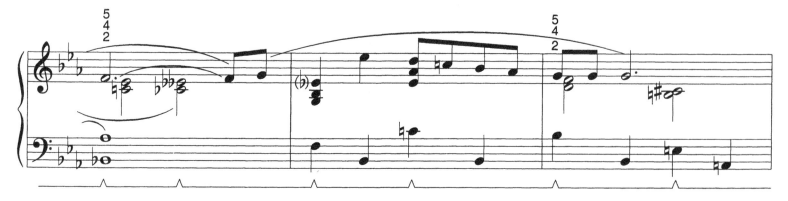

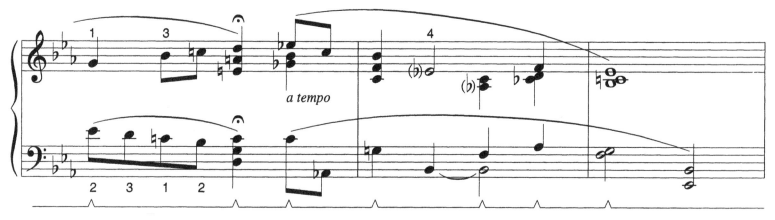

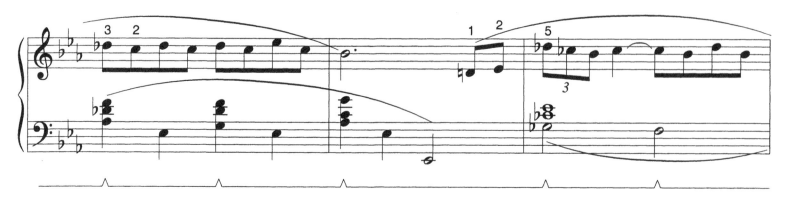

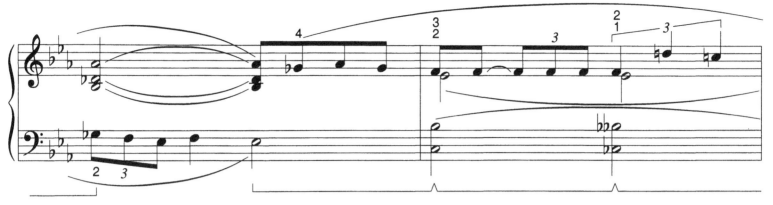

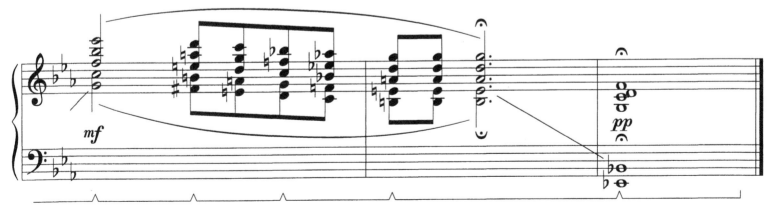

SILVER BELLS
from the Paramount Picture THE LEMON DROP KID

Words and Music by JAY LIVINGSTON
and RAY EVANS
Arranged by LEE EVANS

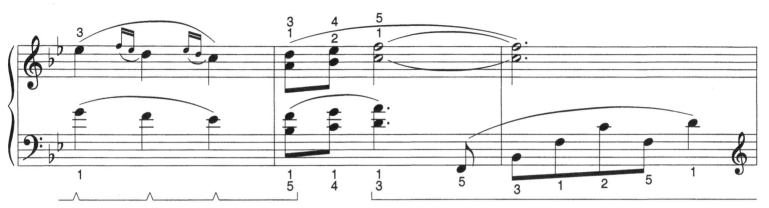
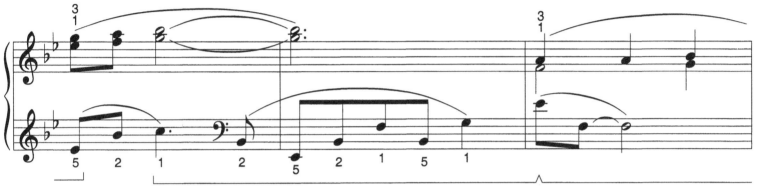
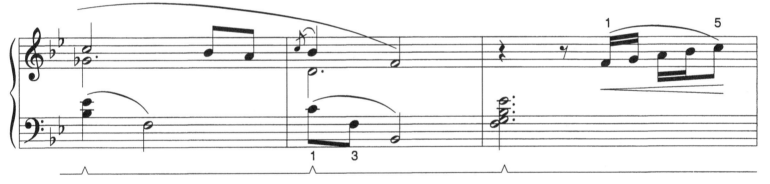
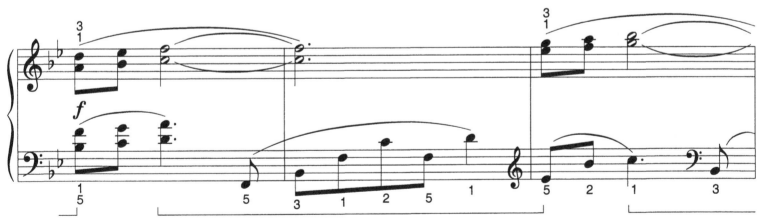
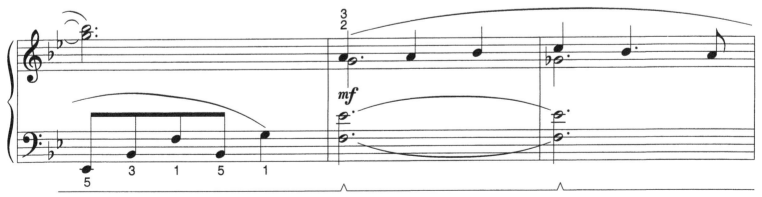

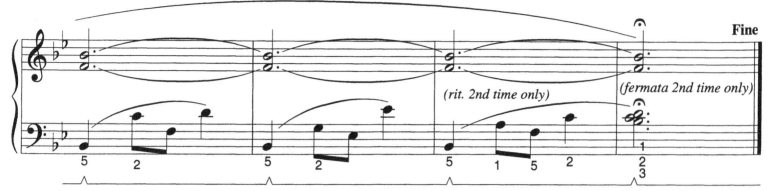

Fine

(rit. 2nd time only) *(fermata 2nd time only)*

Verse

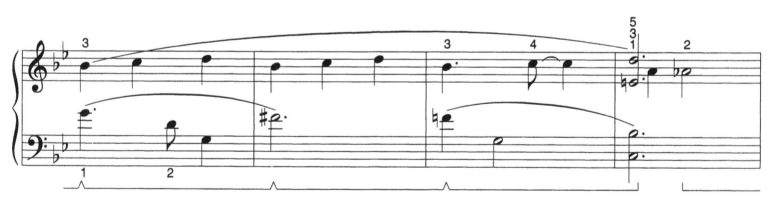

D.S. al Fine (with repeat)

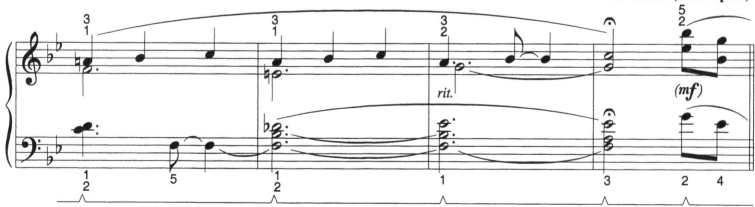

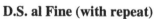

rit. *(mf)*

(THERE'S NO PLACE LIKE)
HOME FOR THE HOLIDAYS

Words by AL STILLMAN
Music by ROBERT ALLEN
Arranged by LEE EVANS

Moderato, rubato

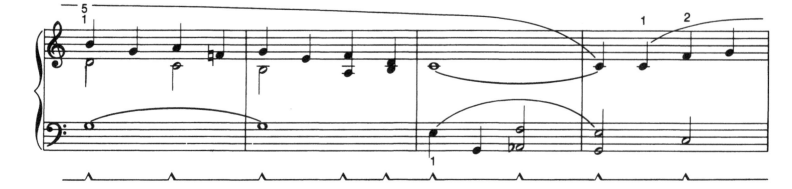

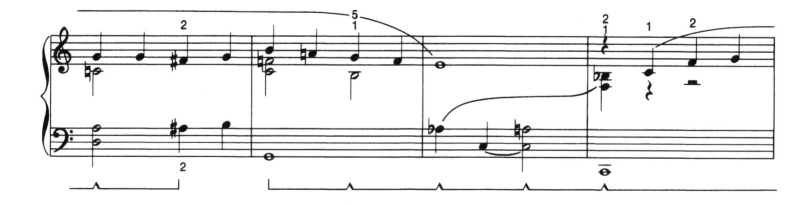

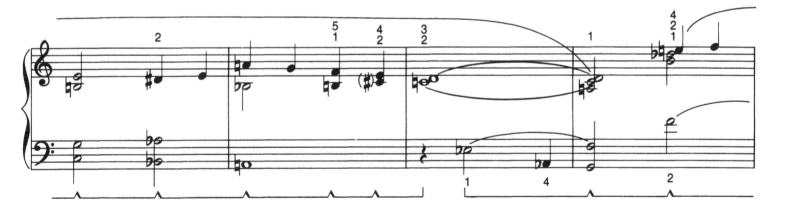

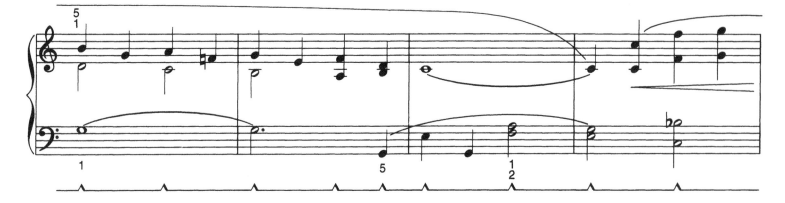

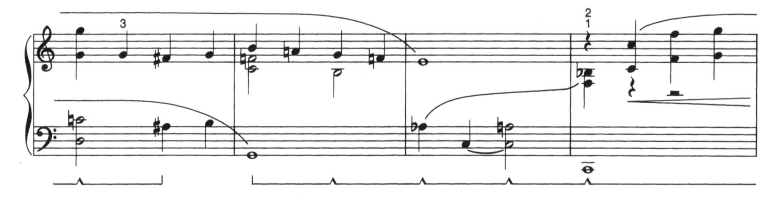

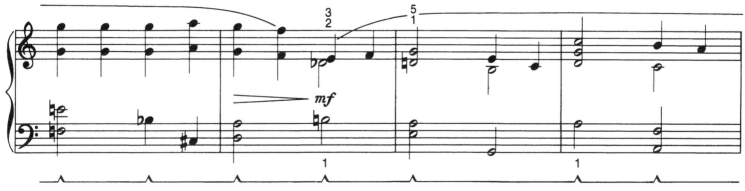

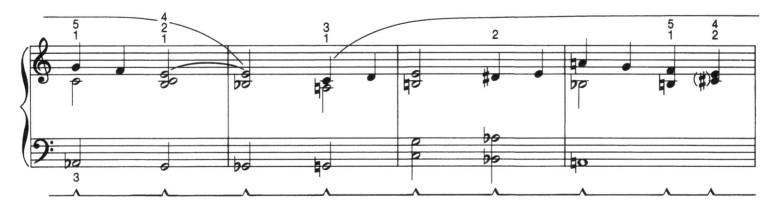

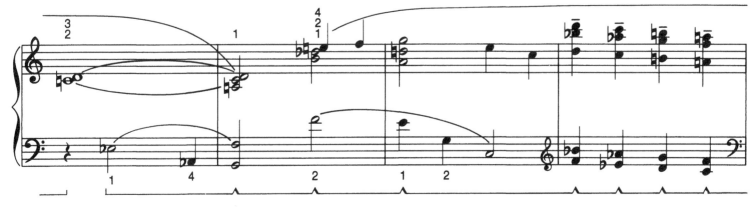

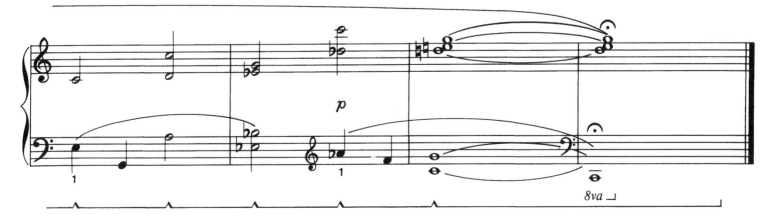

THE CHRISTMAS WALTZ

Words by SAMMY CAHN
Music by JULE STYNE
Arranged by LEE EVANS

Moderately, rubato, with expression

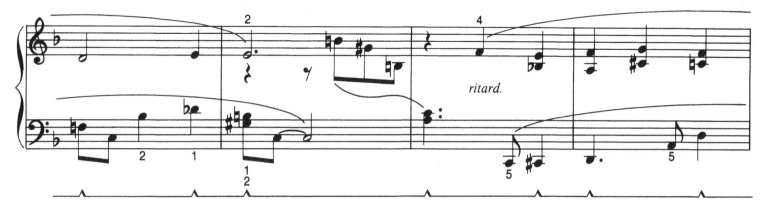

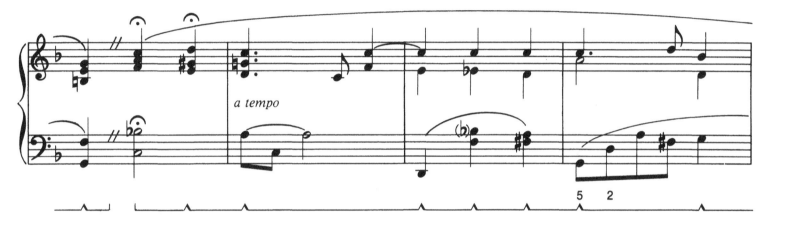

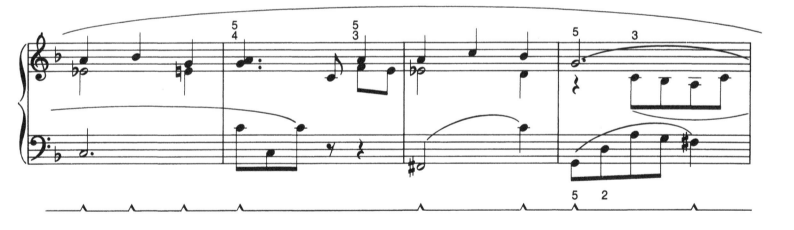

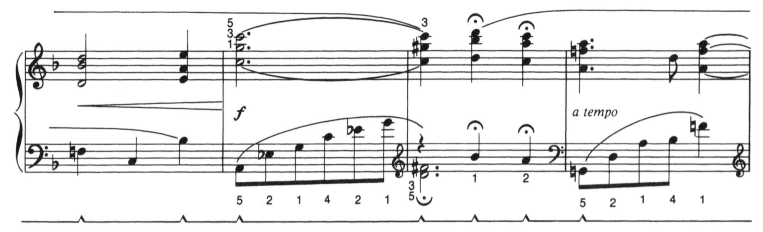

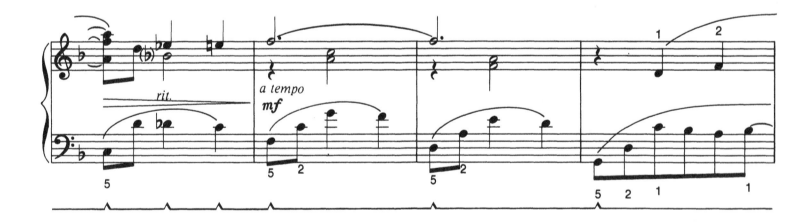

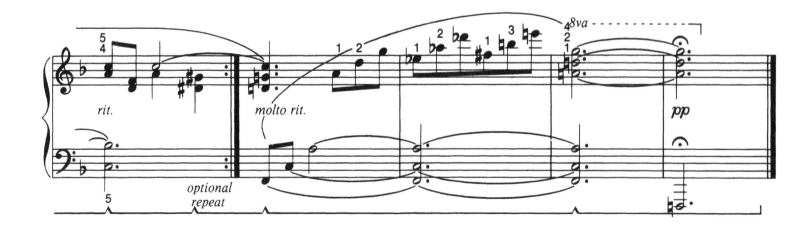

A MARSHMALLOW WORLD

Words by CARL SIGMAN
Music by PETER DE ROSE
Arranged by LEE EVANS

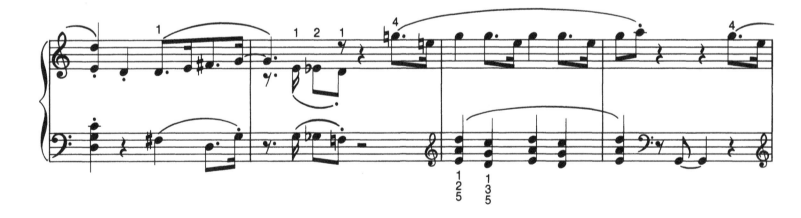

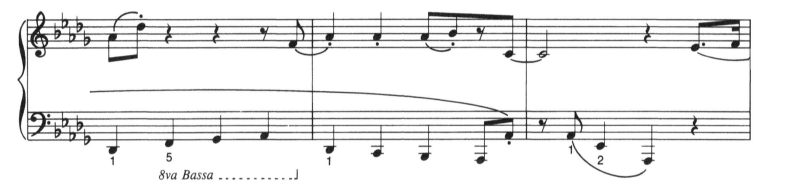

8va Bassa _ _ _ _ _ _ _ _ _ _ _ ⌐

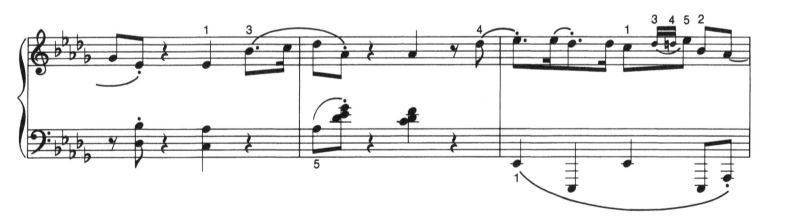

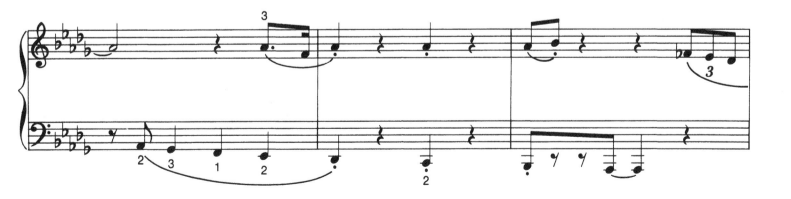

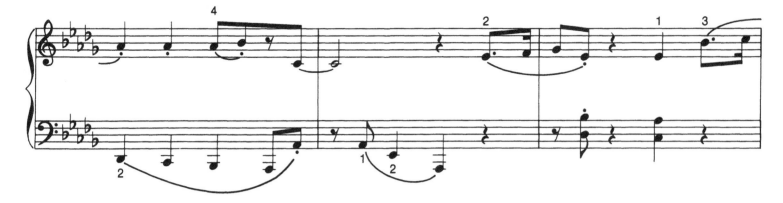

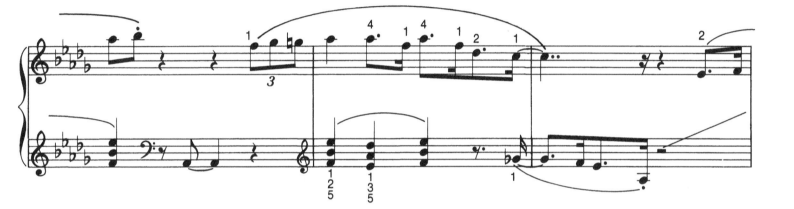

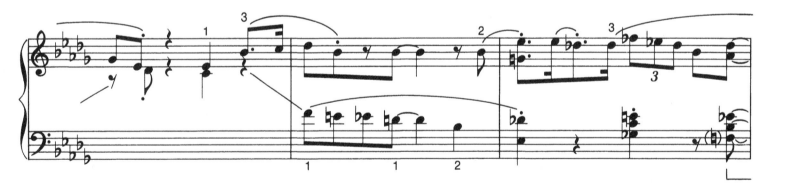

FELIZ NAVIDAD

Music and Lyrics by
JOSE FELICIANO
Arranged by LEE EVANS

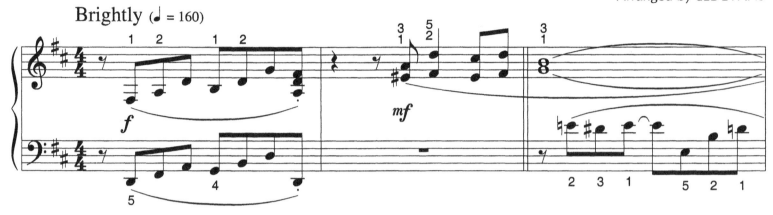

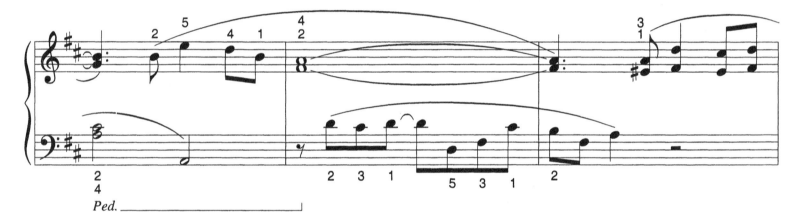

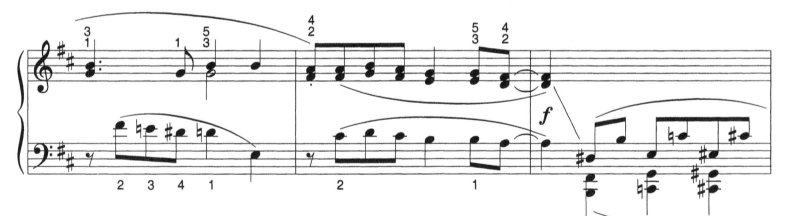

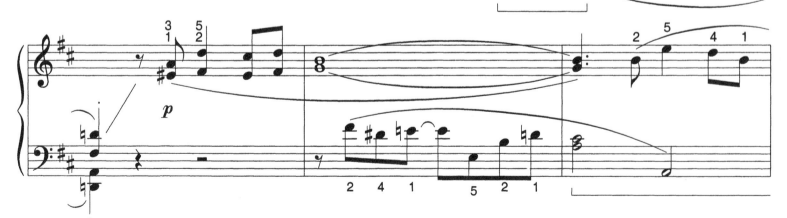

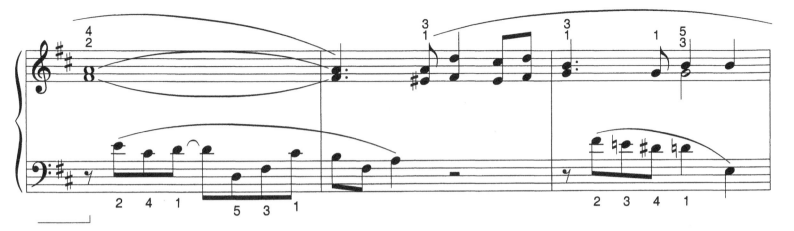

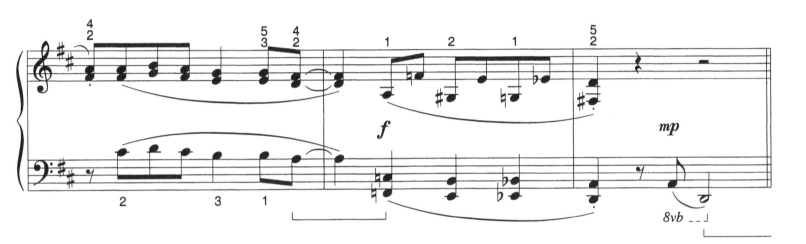

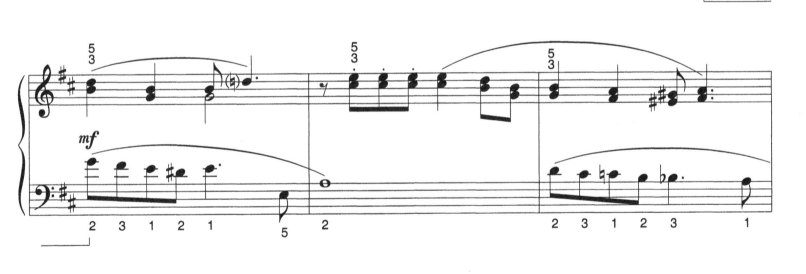

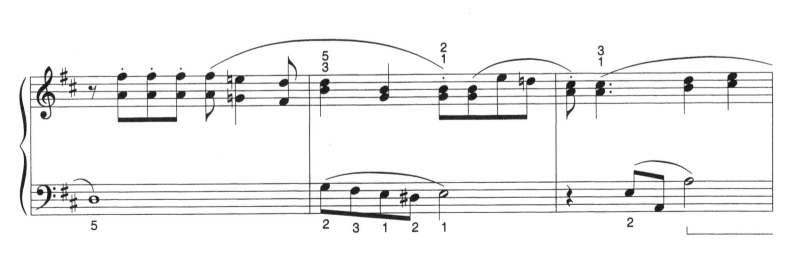

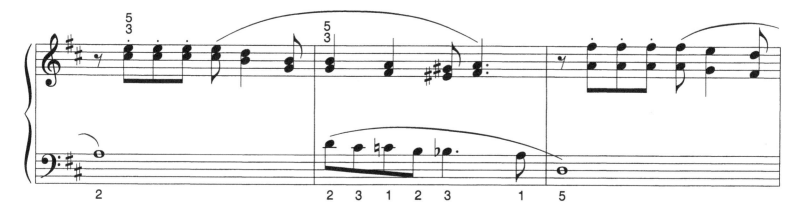

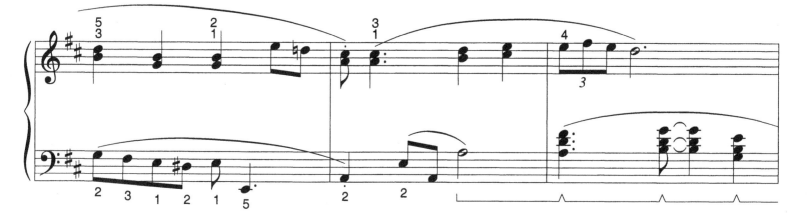

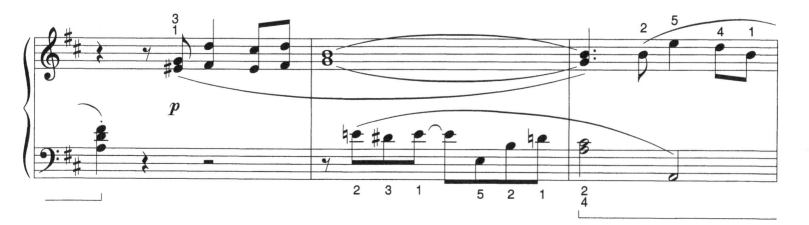

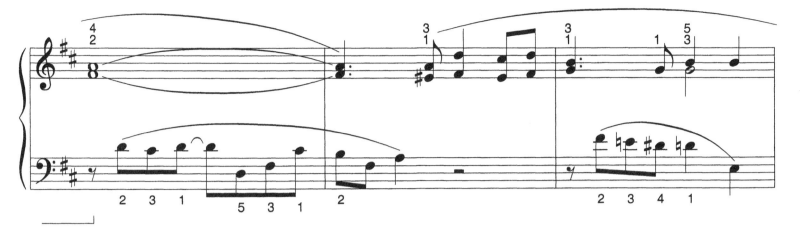

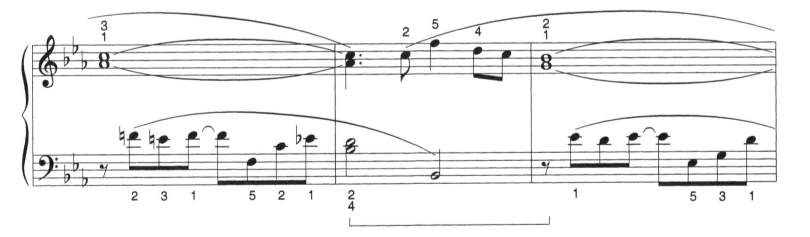

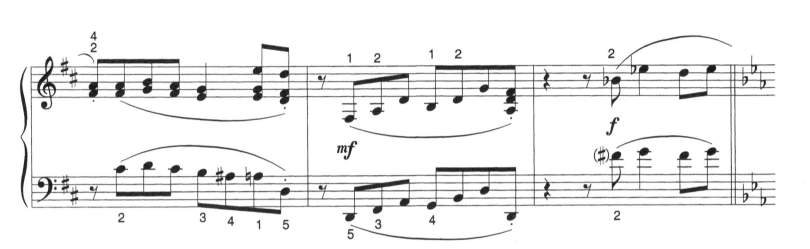

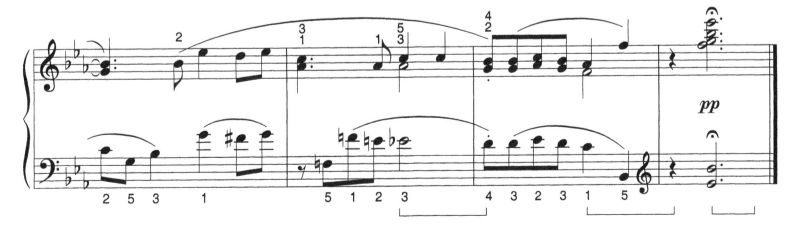

I'LL BE HOME FOR CHRISTMAS

Words and Music by KIM GANNON
and WALTER KENT
Arranged by LEE EVANS

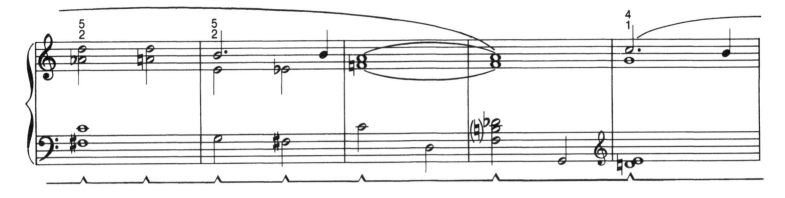

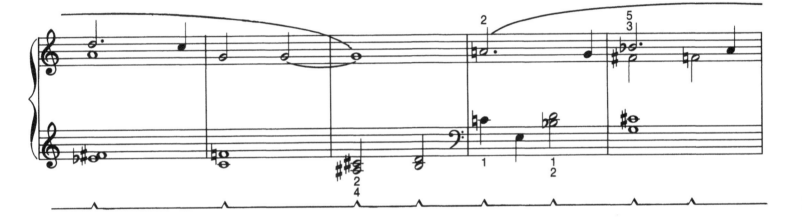

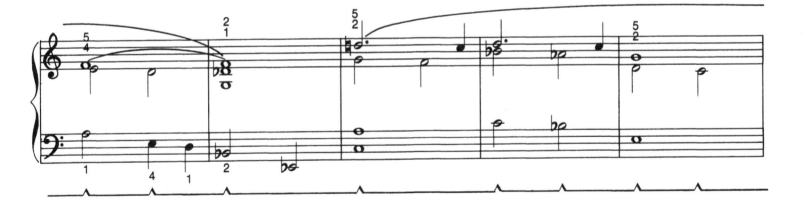

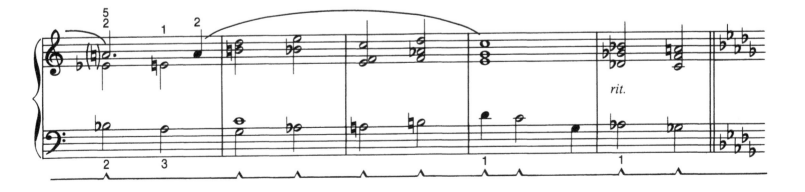

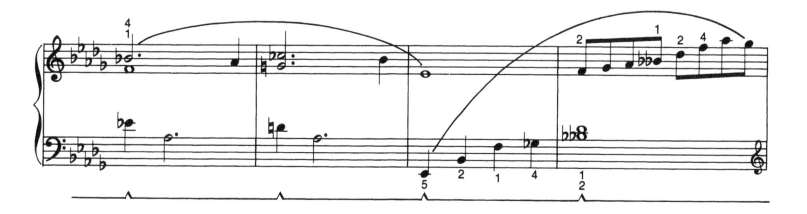

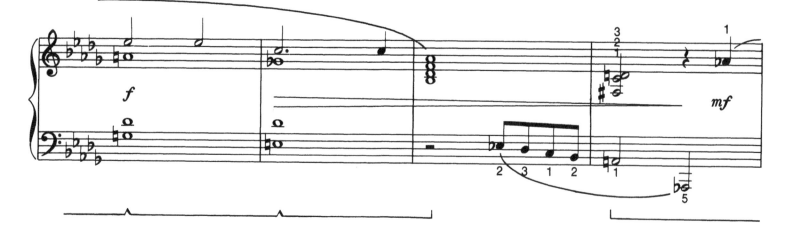

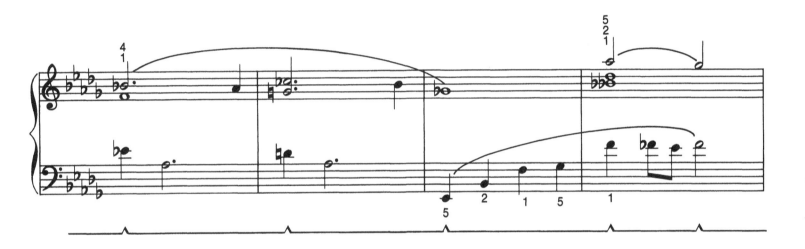

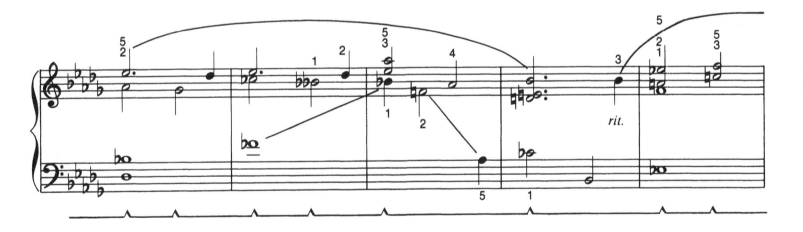

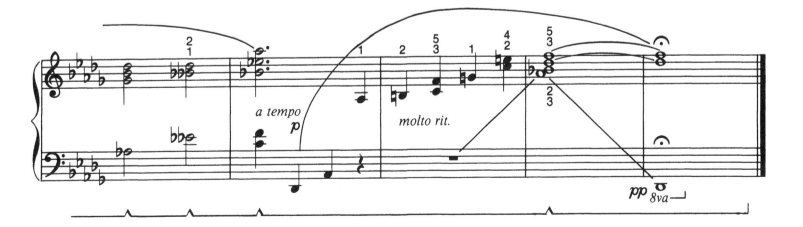

CAROLING, CAROLING

Words by WIHLA HUTSON
Music by ALFRED BURT
Arranged by LEE EVANS

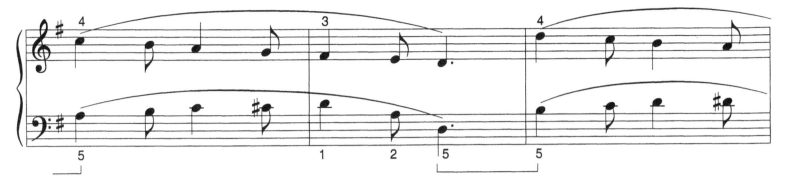

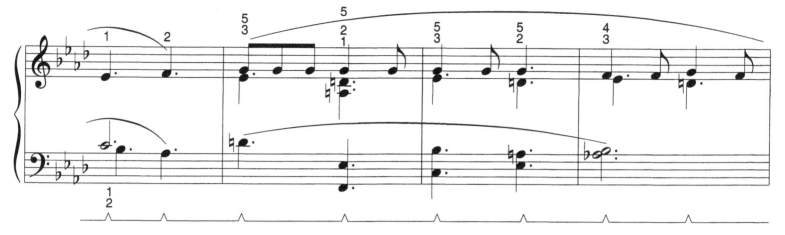

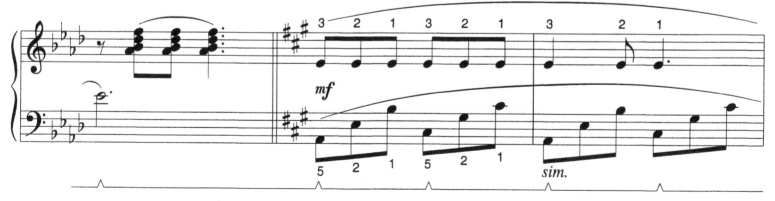

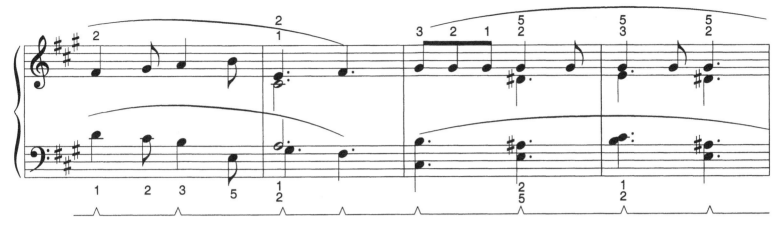

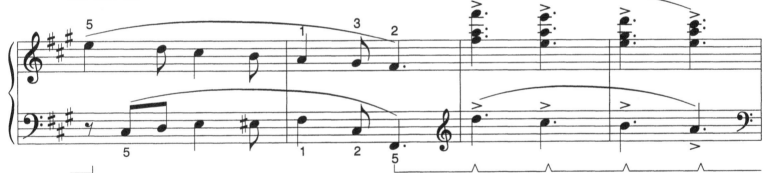

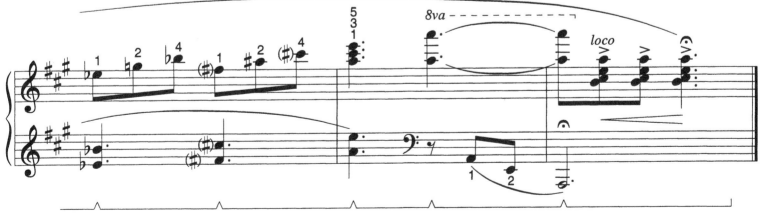

FROSTY THE SNOW MAN

Words and Music by STEVE NELSON
and JACK ROLLINS
Arranged by LEE EVANS

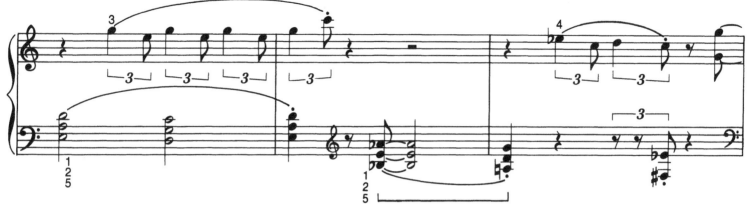

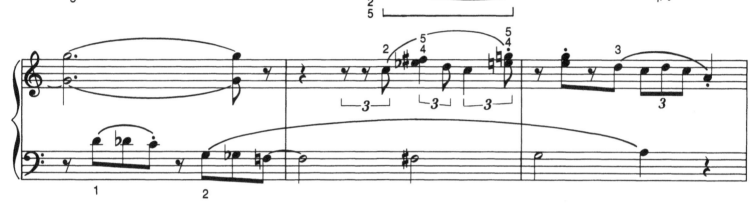

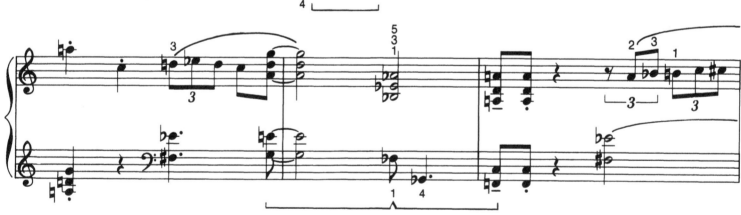

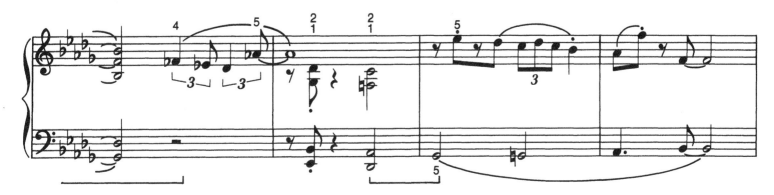

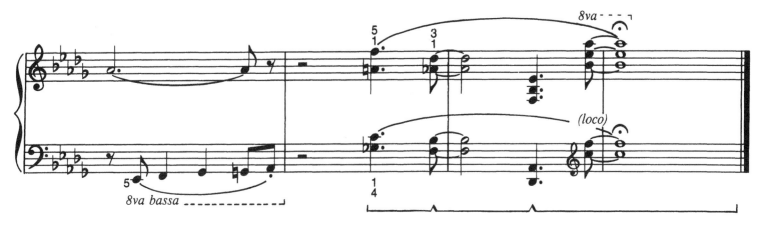

LET IT SNOW! LET IT SNOW! LET IT SNOW!

Words by SAMMY CAHN
Music by JULE STYNE
Arranged by LEE EVANS

Happily (♩ = 144)

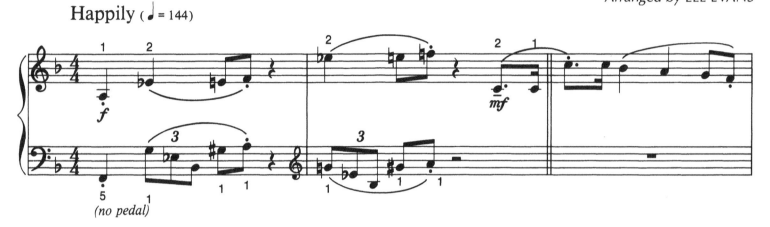

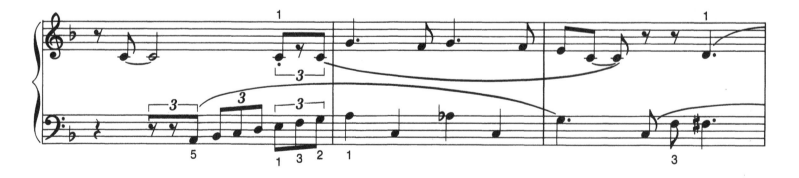

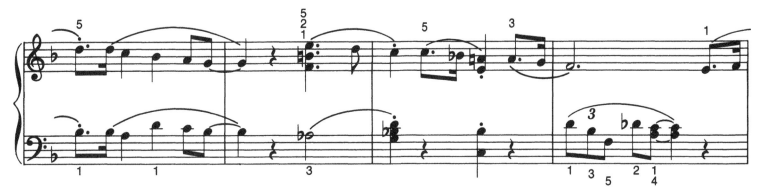

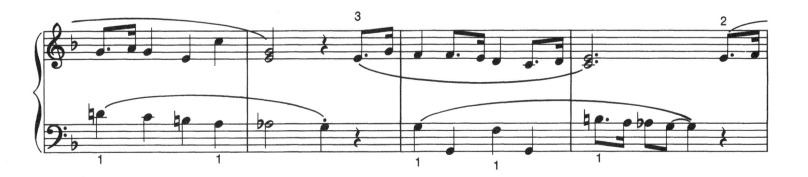

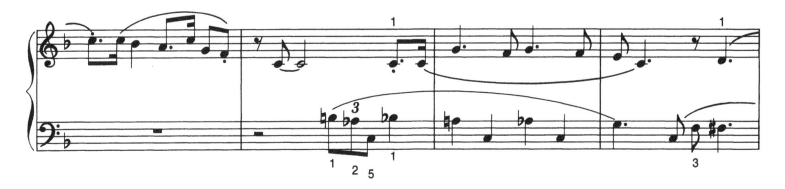

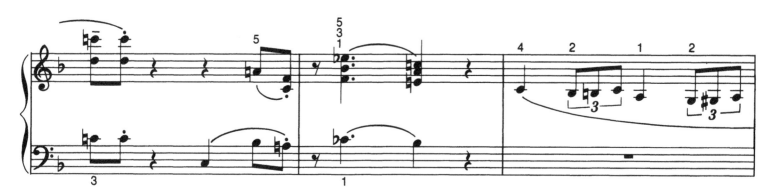

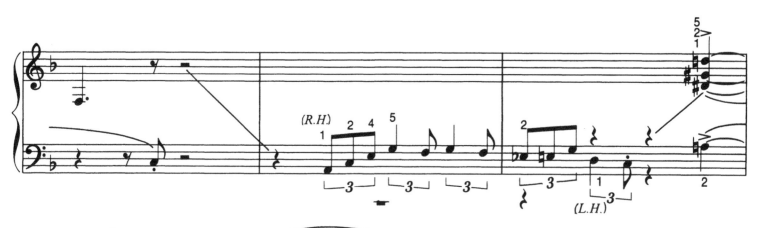

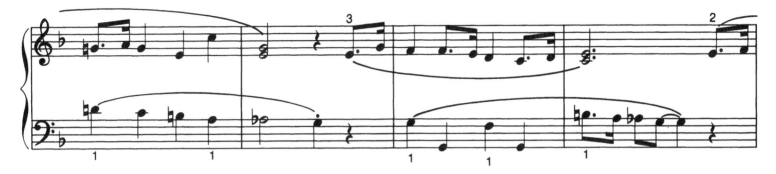

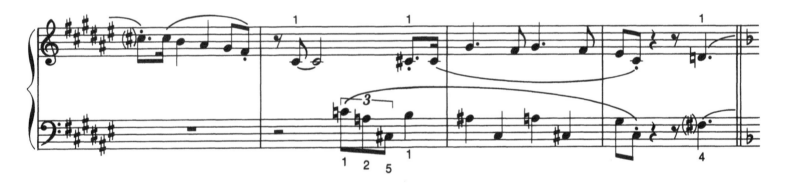

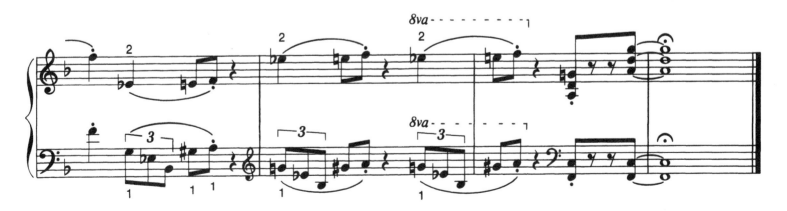

MY FAVORITE THINGS

from THE SOUND OF MUSIC

Lyrics by OSCAR HAMMERSTEIN II
Music by RICHARD RODGERS
Arranged by LEE EVANS

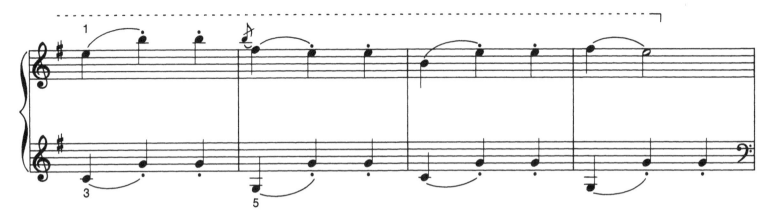

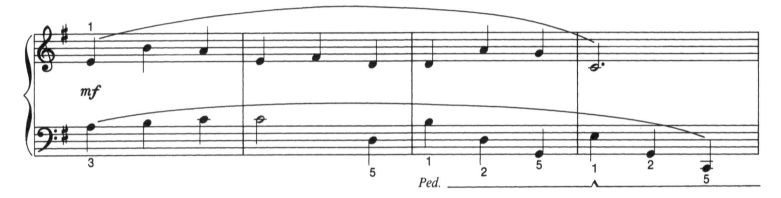

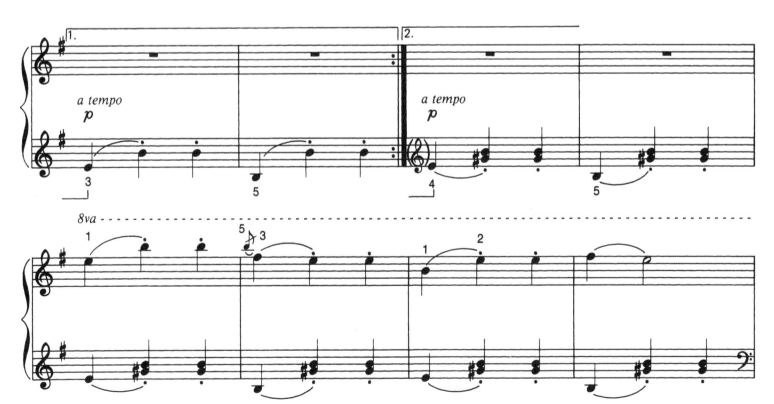

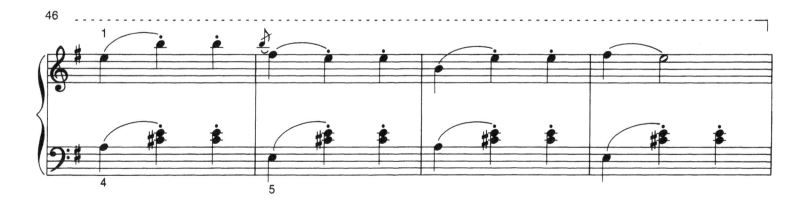

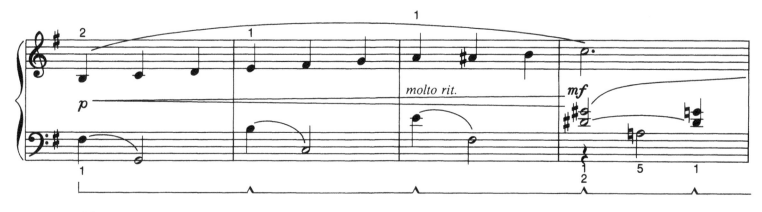

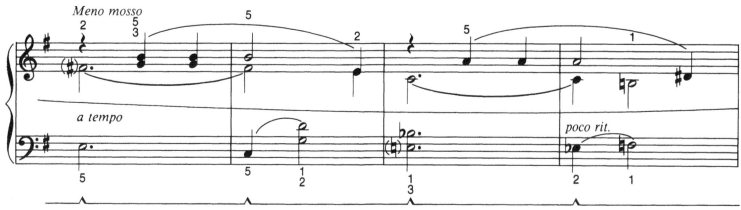

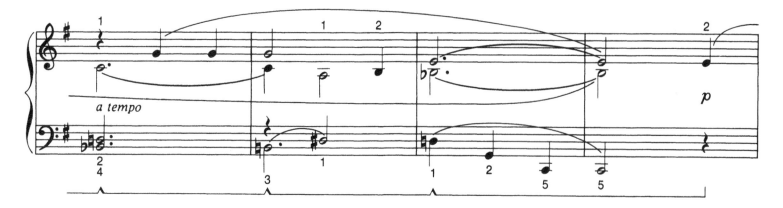

Tempo I

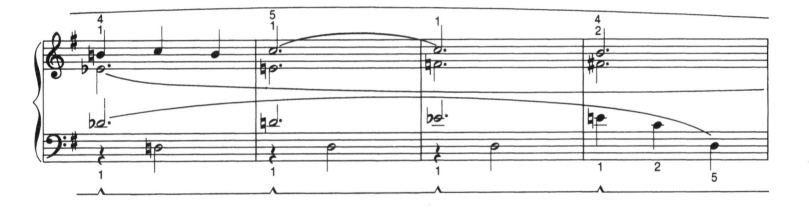

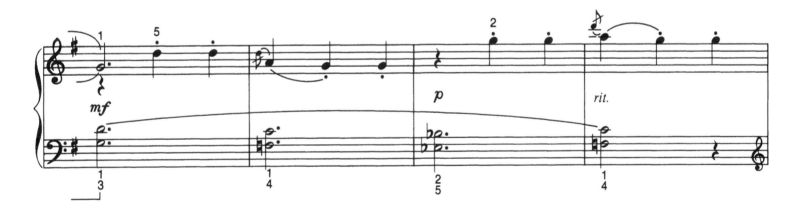

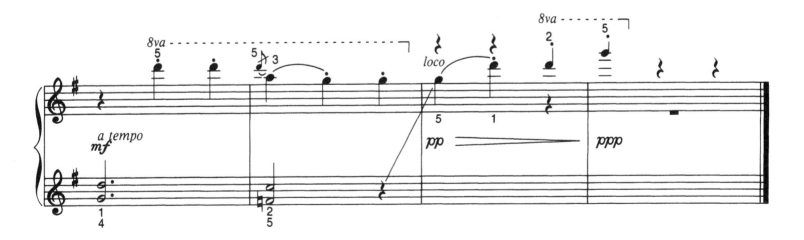